RIO DE JANEIRO
TRAVEL GUIDE 2023:

A Must-Visit Destination for Every Traveler

Max D. Jetsetter

Table of Contents

Introduction

Why Travel to Rio de Janeiro?
What to Expect from Your Trip
History of Rio de Janeiro
Culture and Customs
Religion and Spirituality
Geography and Climate

Chapter 1
Planning Your Trip
When to go
How Long to Stay
Budgeting and Money Tips
Language and Communication
Visa Requirements and Customs
Itinerary Planning

Chapter 2
Top Attractions
1. Christ the Redeemer Statue

2. Sugarloaf Mountain
3. Copacabana Beach
4. Ipanema Beach
5. The Selaron Steps
6. The Botanical Garden
7. The Maracana Stadium
8. The Rio Carnival

Chapter 3
Where to Stay
Accommodation Options
Tips for Finding the Best Deals

Chapter 4
Food and Drink
Brazilian Cuisine and Specialties
Top Restaurants and Bars in Rio de Janeiro
Street Food and Snacks
Vegetarian and Vegan Options

Chapter 5
Nightlife and Entertainment
Clubs, Bars, and Music Venues
Live Music and Performances

Cultural Events and Festivals

Chapter 6
Outdoor Activities
Hiking and Nature Walks
Surfing and Beach Sports
Hang Gliding and Paragliding
Sailing and Boating
Day Trips & Excursions

Chapter 7
Shopping
Local Markets and Street Vendors
Shopping Malls and Department Store
Souvenirs and Gifts

Chapter 8
Transportation
Getting to and From Rio de Janeiro
Traveling About the City via Public Transport
Taxis and ride-sharing services
Hiring a Vehicle or Bike

Chapter 9
Safety and Health
General Safety Recommendations for Travelers
Health and Medical Services
Emergency Contacts and Resources

Chapter 10
Tips for Travelers
General Safety Recommendations for Travelers
Cultural Etiquette and Norms
Essential Portuguese Phrases:
Packing Advice & Recommendations
Dos and Don'ts

Conclusion

Introduction

Welcome to Rio de Janeiro, Brazil! This dynamic metropolis, often known as the "Marvelous City," is a renowned tourism destination that draws millions of people every year. As we commence our Rio de Janeiro travel guidebook for 2023, I will take you on a trip to see the finest of what this city has to offer.

Situated in the southern portion of Brazil, Rio de Janeiro is famed for its magnificent beaches, unique culture, wonderful cuisine, and bustling nightlife. From the renowned Christ the Redeemer monument to the vibrant Carnival events, there is no lack of things to do and see in this busy metropolis.

When you start your tour in Rio de Janeiro, you will note the unique combination of contemporary and traditional components that make up the city's ambiance. The city is home to a varied population, which has molded the culture and traditions that make Rio de Janeiro a must-visit destination.

Whether you're a first-time tourist or a returning traveler, this guidebook will provide you with all the information you need to make the most of your stay in Rio de Janeiro. We'll cover everything from the greatest locations to stay, the most delicious meals to taste, the top tourist sites, and the most interesting activities to indulge in.

In this guidebook, I'll also emphasize the safety measures you need to take while touring the city, as well as recommendations on how to navigate about the city with ease. I want you to have the greatest experience possible in Rio de Janeiro and be able to make the most of your stay in the city.

I hope this guidebook will serve as a valuable resource as you plan your vacation to Rio de Janeiro. From the sun-kissed beaches to the busy nightlife, Rio de Janeiro offers something for everyone. So pack your luggage, grab your sunscreen, and get ready to explore the enchantment of this magnificent city!

Why Travel to Rio de Janeiro?

Rio de Janeiro, usually known as Rio, is one of the most renowned and popular places in Brazil. The city is widely recognized for its magnificent beaches, active culture, and breathtaking natural beauty, making it an excellent destination for travelers from all over the globe. Whether you are an adventure seeker, a cultural enthusiast, or just seeking a quiet break, Rio de Janeiro has plenty to offer everyone. **These are some reasons why you might consider visiting Rio de Janeiro:**

Beaches
Rio de Janeiro is home to some of the most stunning beaches in the world. The most renowned beach in Rio is Copacabana Beach, a four-kilometer strip of white sand that draws millions of visitors every year. Other prominent beaches in Rio are Ipanema Beach, Leblon Beach, and Barra da Tijuca Beach, each giving a distinct experience. Guests may sunbathe, swim, surf, or just enjoy the spectacular views of the ocean.

Culture and History
Rio de Janeiro is a city with a rich cultural and historical legacy. The city is home to various museums, including the National Museum of Brazil, the Museum of Modern Art, and the Museum of the Republic. The city also boasts a thriving music and dance culture, with samba being the most popular dance genre. Tourists may experience the vivid

culture of Rio by watching a samba performance, visiting a favela (a Brazilian shantytown), or taking part in the city's famed Carnival festivities.

Natural Beauty

Rio de Janeiro is a city surrounded by natural beauty. The city is located on Guanabara Bay and is surrounded by beautiful mountains, including the famed Sugarloaf Peak and Corcovado Mountain, home to the iconic Christ the Redeemer monument. Tourists may take a cable car to the summit of Sugarloaf Peak or a train to the top of Corcovado Mountain for beautiful views of the city and the surrounding area.

Food and Drink

Brazilian food is a combination of African, European, and Indigenous traditions, making it distinctive and delectable. Rio de Janeiro is famed for its traditional Brazilian cuisine such as feijoada, a substantial stew made with black beans and pork, and churrasco, a barbecue-style dish. Tourists may also enjoy fresh seafood, tropical fruits, and unique drinks while taking in the city's exciting nightlife.

Sports

Rio de Janeiro has a love for sports, with soccer being the most popular sport in the city. Tourists may see a game at the iconic Maracanã Stadium, one of the biggest soccer stadiums in the world. The city is also recognized for its water activities, including surfing, windsurfing, and kiteboarding.

Rio de Janeiro is a location that provides a unique combination of natural beauty, culture, and history. Tourists may enjoy magnificent beaches, colorful music and dancing, wonderful food and drink, and a love for sports. Rio de Janeiro is a must-visit place for anybody searching for an amazing experience in Brazil.

What to Expect from Your Trip

Rio de Janeiro is a dynamic and colorful metropolis situated on Brazil's southern coast. It's a popular site for travelers from all over the globe, and with good reason. Rio is recognized for its magnificent beaches, bustling nightlife, and rich cultural legacy.

Here's what you can anticipate from your vacation to Rio de Janeiro:

Gorgeous Beaches
One of the biggest charms of Rio de Janeiro is its magnificent beaches. Copacabana is possibly the most renowned of them, with its long length of golden sand and blue ocean. Ipanema and Leblon are equally renowned beaches, recognized for their gorgeous surroundings and vibrant ambiance. There are lots of coastal pubs and restaurants where you can relax and soak up the sun.

Iconic Landmarks
Rio de Janeiro is home to some renowned sites that are worth seeing. Among the most renowned of them is the Christ the Redeemer monument, which lies atop Corcovado Mountain and affords breathtaking views of the city. The Sugarloaf Mountain cable car is another famous attraction, transporting tourists up to the summit of Sugarloaf Mountain for panoramic views of the city.

Exciting Nightlife
Rio de Janeiro is renowned for its active nightlife, with lots of pubs, clubs, and music venues to pick

from. Lapa is a renowned district for nightlife, with its bustling street parties and samba clubs. If you're searching for a more affluent experience, travel to the district of Leblon, which is home to numerous high-end clubs and restaurants.

Delicious Food

Brazilian food is famed for its robust tastes and fresh ingredients, and Rio de Janeiro is no exception. Some of the must-try delicacies in Rio are feijoada (a hearty stew made with beans and pork), churrasco (Brazilian-style BBQ), and coxinha (deep-fried chicken balls) (deep-fried chicken balls). You'll find lots of eateries dishing up wonderful Brazilian meals across the city.

Rich Cultural Heritage

Rio de Janeiro is deep in history and culture, and there are lots of museums and sites to visit. The Museum of Future, situated in the port sector, is a must-visit for anybody interested in science and technology. The National Museum of Brazil is another famous site, presenting Brazil's rich cultural legacy via its exhibitions.

Festivals and Events

Rio de Janeiro is recognized for its bright and vivid festivals and festivities. Arguably the most renowned of them is Carnival, which takes place in February and is a tremendous festival of music, dancing, and culture. Other notable events include the Rock in Rio music festival, the Rio International Film Festival, and the New Year's Eve festivities on Copacabana Beach.

A vacation to Rio de Janeiro promises to be a memorable experience packed with magnificent beaches, famous monuments, thrilling nightlife, wonderful cuisine, rich culture, and vibrant festivals and events. Whether you're a first-time visitor or a seasoned tourist, there's always something new to discover in this gorgeous city.

History of Rio de Janeiro

Rio de Janeiro is one of the most recognized and recognizable towns in Brazil, noted for its magnificent natural beauty, rich culture, and dynamic lifestyle. The city is a melting pot of history, architecture, and varied traditions that have been impacted by centuries of colonialism, wars, and social and political movements.

Rio de Janeiro was founded in 1565 by the Portuguese explorer Estácio de Sá, who created the city as a strategic center for the Portuguese colonization of Brazil. The city was originally called São Sebastião do Rio de Janeiro, in honor of Saint Sebastian and the natural bay of Rio de Janeiro.

During colonial times, Rio de Janeiro became an important port for the commerce of gold, diamonds, and other precious goods. The city was also the headquarters of the Portuguese royal court during the early 19th century, when Napoleon's army invaded Portugal, compelling the Portuguese king to escape to Brazil.

In 1808, the Portuguese royal family landed in Rio de Janeiro, making the city into the capital of the Portuguese Empire. This event was a turning point in the history of Rio de Janeiro, as the city underwent a period of economic prosperity, cultural interaction, and urban development.

During this era, Rio de Janeiro became the cultural hub of Brazil, drawing authors, painters, musicians, and intellectuals from all around the nation. The city also experienced the rise of new architectural forms, including neoclassicism and art nouveau, which can still be seen in many of the city's renowned structures, including the Theatro Municipal, the National Library of Brazil, and the Municipal Chamber.

Throughout the 20th century, Rio de Janeiro continued to grow as a cultural and commercial center, although confronting numerous social and political obstacles. In 1960, the capital of Brazil was transferred to Brasília, leading Rio de Janeiro to lose part of its political significance, but the city remained a lively hub of art, music, and culture.

Throughout the 1970s and 1980s, Rio de Janeiro was devastated by a surge of violence and crime, driven by drug trafficking and urban poverty. These concerns culminated in the 1990s with the establishment of strong drug cartels that ruled many of the city's favelas (slums) and generated a wave of violence that lasted for years.

Nowadays, Rio de Janeiro has seen substantial changes, with advances in public security, urban infrastructure, and social initiatives. The city continues to be a significant cultural hub, holding events including the Carnival and the Rock in Rio music festival, and drawing millions of visitors each year.

Visitors to Rio de Janeiro may discover the city's rich history and cultural legacy by visiting its numerous museums, art galleries, and historic sites, such as the Christ the Redeemer statue, Sugarloaf Mountain, and the Copacabana Palace Hotel. Visitors may also experience the rich and varied culture of the city by visiting its neighborhoods, experiencing its food, and enjoying its music and nightlife.

Culture and Customs

Rio de Janeiro is one of the most popular places in Brazil. Yet, before visiting this magnificent city, it is vital to learn its distinct culture and traditions.

Following are some features of Rio de Janeiro's culture and traditions that tourists should know:

Language: Portuguese is the official language of Brazil, and although many people in Rio de Janeiro speak English, it is always a good idea to learn some basic Portuguese phrases before going. This will not only aid with communication but also show respect for the local culture.

Food and Drink: Brazilian food is a combination of European, African, and indigenous influences, resulting in a diversified and rich meal. Visitors visiting Rio de Janeiro should enjoy typical delicacies such as Feijoada (a black bean stew with pork), Pão de Queijo (cheese bread), and Brigadeiro (a chocolate dessert) (a chocolate dessert). Brazil is also renowned for its coffee and Caipirinha, a popular drink composed with cachaça, sugar, and lime.

Music and Dance: Samba is a popular music and dance style in Rio de Janeiro, and tourists may experience it in the city's numerous nightclubs and during the annual Carnival carnival. Other prominent music genres include funk carioca, pagode, and forró.

Religion: Brazil is largely a Catholic nation, although other faiths such as Protestantism, Spiritism, and Afro-Brazilian religions are also widespread in Rio de Janeiro. Visitors should be mindful of religious norms and dress modestly while visiting churches and other religious places.

Festivals and Celebrations: Rio de Janeiro is recognized for its colorful festivals, the most famous of which is the Carnival, held in February or March. During Carnival, the city comes alive with parades, costumes, and music. Guests should book their accommodation well in advance during this period since it is a popular event. Other events in Rio de Janeiro include the Festa Junina (a celebration of St. John's Day) and the Reveillon (New Year's Eve).

Social Customs: Brazilians are famed for their friendliness and hospitality, and tourists visiting Rio de Janeiro may expect to be welcomed with embraces and kisses on the cheek. It is also normal for individuals to come late to social occasions, therefore it is good to have a flexible approach towards timeliness. Tipping is usual at restaurants and for services such as haircuts.

Safety: Like any major city, Rio de Janeiro has certain safety problems, therefore tourists should take steps to protect their safety. It is advisable to avoid carrying valuables in public, to use only licensed taxis, and to be mindful of your surroundings at all times.

Rio de Janeiro is a diversified and culturally rich city that is full of life and excitement. Visitors who take the time to learn about the local culture and traditions will have a more rewarding and delightful experience in this lovely city.

Religion and Spirituality

Rio de Janeiro is a city that is profoundly immersed in both religion and spirituality. As a tourist, you will encounter a complex tapestry of beliefs and customs that are still observed and enjoyed by the inhabitants.

One of the most important faiths in Rio de Janeiro is Catholicism, which was brought by the Portuguese invaders in the 16th century. The city includes a variety of ancient churches, including the famed Christ the Redeemer monument that overlooks the city from the summit of Corcovado Mountain. The Catedral Metropolitana, with its characteristic conical design, is well worth seeing. These religious structures are not only noteworthy for their historical and architectural value, but also as places of worship for the fervent Catholic population of Rio.

Another important religion in Rio de Janeiro is Candomblé, which is an Afro-Brazilian religion that integrates aspects of Catholicism, African animism, and indigenous mysticism. Candomblé is a syncretic religion that has been practiced in Brazil since the 19th century and is marked by its loud song, dancing, and colorful rites. Visitors may enjoy Candomblé rites in several of the city's terreiros (religious homes), but it's crucial to follow the traditions and conventions of this very spiritual and intimate religion.

Umbanda is another syncretic religion that is followed in Rio de Janeiro, which incorporates parts of African faiths, indigenous traditions, and Spiritism (a spiritualist ideology that emerged in France in the 19th century) (a spiritualist philosophy that originated in France in the 19th century). Umbanda is recognized for its use of mediums, who are supposed to interact with spirits to bring direction and healing to believers. Visitors may enjoy Umbanda rites in several of the city's terreiros, but once again, it's crucial to be polite and open-minded to the spiritual beliefs of others.

Spirituality in Rio de Janeiro is not restricted to organized faiths, but also encompasses the activities of various spiritualists and mystics. One such example is the work of John of God, a prominent Brazilian medium who has developed a global following for his healing work. Tourists may visit John of God's facility in Abadiânia, a little hamlet outside of Rio de Janeiro, to observe his healing work firsthand.

In addition to these official faiths and spiritual activities, Rio de Janeiro is also recognized for its lively Carnival festivities, which are profoundly steeped in both religion and spirituality. Carnival is observed in the days leading up to Lent, and it is a time when people gather together to dance, sing, and celebrate life. The carnival is a spectacle of song, dancing, and spectacular costumes, and it is heavily inspired by the religious traditions of Brazil.

Ultimately, Rio de Janeiro is a city that is entrenched in both religion and spirituality. As a guest, it's crucial to be respectful of the beliefs and customs of the people and to approach these rituals with an open mind and heart. Whether you're interested in visiting old churches, experiencing Candomblé or Umbanda rites, or partaking in the exuberant Carnival festivities, Rio de Janeiro provides a rich and varied spiritual environment that is worth investigating.

Geography and Climate

Rio de Janeiro is a city situated in the southern portion of Brazil, recognized for its spectacular natural landscapes, cultural variety, and active nightlife. The city enjoys a pleasant tropical environment, with temperatures that are generally stable throughout the year, making it a great location for those seeking sunlight and mild weather.

Geography:

Rio de Janeiro is located on the Atlantic coast of Brazil, having a total land area of 1,255.3 km². The city is surrounded by beautiful mountains, notably the famed Corcovado Mountain, which includes the iconic Cristo Redentor (Christ the Redeemer) monument. The city is also home to numerous gorgeous beaches, including Copacabana, Ipanema, and Leblon, which draw people from all over the globe.

Climate:

Rio de Janeiro has a tropical climate, with moderate temperatures and high humidity levels year-round. The city has two different seasons: a rainy season from December to March, and a dry season from June to September. During the rainy season, tourists may anticipate regular rains, while temperatures remain mild, with highs averaging approximately 30°C (86°F). The dry season is marked by sunny days and moderate temperatures, with typical highs about 26°C (79°F).

Owing to its position near the equator, Rio de Janeiro has only slight fluctuations in temperature throughout the year. Nonetheless, tourists should be advised that the city may be impacted by tropical storms and hurricanes, especially during the rainy season. It is crucial to watch weather forecasts and follow local recommendations to maintain personal safety during these incidents.

Rio de Janeiro's distinctive terrain and mild tropical climate make it a perfect location for those seeking sun, beach, and gorgeous natural scenery. Whether you're visiting the city's ancient buildings, soaking up the sun on its stunning beaches, or trekking through its lush woods, Rio de Janeiro provides something for everyone. Just remember to remain safe and follow local advice during the city's infrequent tropical storms and hurricanes.

Chapter 1

Planning Your Trip

Situated on Brazil's Atlantic coast, Rio de Janeiro is recognized for its magnificent beaches, outstanding architecture, active music and dance scene, and unique cultural sites. Whether you're interested in discovering the city's colonial history, soaking up the sun on its world-famous beaches, or immersing yourself in its vibrant street culture, Rio de Janeiro offers something for everyone.

But, arranging a vacation to this crowded metropolis may be intimidating, particularly for first-time tourists. In this guide, I'll present you with some crucial ideas and information to help you plan your trip to Rio de Janeiro and make the most of your stay in this great city. From the ideal time to travel to top sites to see, I've got you covered. Now, grab a caipirinha and let's get started!

When to go

With its magnificent beaches, active nightlife, and renowned sites such as Christ the Redeemer and Sugarloaf Mountain, Rio de Janeiro is a must-visit destination for everyone going to Brazil. Nevertheless, what is the ideal time to visit Rio de Janeiro as a visitor?

Weather-wise, Rio de Janeiro is noted for its hot and humid environment, with temperatures varying from 25 to 35 degrees Celsius (77 to 95 degrees Fahrenheit) throughout the year. The city has two different seasons: the dry season, which runs from May to September, and the rainy season, which goes from October to April.

If you're considering a vacation to Rio de Janeiro, the ideal time to visit is during the dry season. This is when the weather is most pleasant, with reduced humidity and fewer wet days. The dry season is also the main tourist season in Rio de Janeiro, which means that the city is teeming with activity and there are lots of events and festivals to attend.

One of the most popular events during the dry season is Carnaval, which takes place in February or March. Carnaval is a large celebration that lasts for several days and draws millions of people from all over the globe. During Carnaval, the streets of Rio de Janeiro are filled with music, dancing, and bright parades, making it a really unique event.

Another fantastic time to visit Rio de Janeiro is during the offseason, which spans from April to October. During this season, the weather is still good, but there are less visitors, which means that you may experience the city's attractions without the crowds. This is also a wonderful time to get savings on flights and lodgings, since costs tend to be cheaper during the offseason.

Yet, it's crucial to bear in mind that Rio de Janeiro is a popular destination year-round, and there is always something to see and do. Whether you're traveling during the high tourist season or the offseason, there are plenty of things to do in Rio de Janeiro, including its beaches, museums, and cultural icons.

The optimum time to visit Rio de Janeiro as a tourist is during the dry season, which spans from May to

September. This is when the weather is most lovely and there are lots of activities and festivals to attend. Nevertheless, the offseason from April to October might also be a nice time to visit, since costs tend to be cheaper and there are fewer people. Ultimately, the ideal time to visit Rio de Janeiro depends on your interests and travel itinerary, but no matter when you go, you're guaranteed to have an outstanding experience in this dynamic and energetic city.

How Long to Stay

If you are considering a vacation to Rio, one of the issues you may have is how long you should remain in the city. The answer to this question will rely on a variety of things, including your interests, budget, and travel style.

These are some variables to consider while determining how long to stay in Rio de Janeiro:

Your Interests: Rio de Janeiro is a city with a broad range of attractions, and the duration of your visit should depend on what you want to see and do. If you are interested in beaches, you may want to spend more time in Rio to thoroughly explore the various beaches the city has to offer, such as Copacabana, Ipanema, and Leblon. If you are interested in culture and history, you may wish to spend more time visiting museums and historic locations, such as the National Museum of Brazil, the Imperial Museum, and the Santa Teresa area.

Your Budget: The duration of your stay in Rio will also depend on your budget. Rio may be an expensive city to visit, particularly if you want to stay in the more luxury areas. If you are on a limited budget, you may want to restrict your visit to just a few days, since this will allow you enough time to explore some of the top sights without breaking the bank.

Your Travel Style: If you are the sort of traveler who loves to take things easy and fully immerse oneself in a location, you may choose to remain in Rio for a longer amount of time. On the other hand, if you want to travel swiftly from one place to the next, you may be able to see all you want to see in only a few days.

So, how long should you remain in Rio de Janeiro?

For most tourists, a stay of roughly 4-5 days is advised, since this will allow you enough time to explore some of the key sights and acquire a feel for the city. During this time, you may tour the beaches, see the Christ the Redeemer monument, take a cable car trip up to Sugarloaf Mountain, and explore the colorful districts of Santa Teresa and Lapa.

If you have more time to spare, there are lots of additional things to see and do in Rio de Janeiro. For example, you may take a day excursion to the adjacent city of Petropolis, which is noted for its imperial past and attractive architecture. You may also take a boat tour of Guanabara Bay, trek in the Tijuca National Park, or visit some of the city's lesser-known areas, such as Jardim Botanico or Botafogo.

If you have less time to spend, it is still possible to have a flavor of Rio de Janeiro in only a few days. For example, you could spend one day on the beaches, one day touring the major sites, and one day exploring the neighborhoods and enjoying the local food.

The duration of your stay in Rio de Janeiro will depend on your interests, money, and travel style. Yet, regardless of how long you stay, you are bound to be charmed by the beauty and vitality of this dynamic city.

Budgeting and Money Tips

Rio de Janeiro is a lovely city with a rich cultural past and a broad selection of attractions. It is also a somewhat pricey city, particularly for visitors. But, with proper preparation and budgeting, it is feasible to enjoy everything that the city has to offer without breaking the bank. In this section of the guide, I will share some ideas on budgeting and managing money in Rio de Janeiro.

Plan Ahead

Before you fly to Rio de Janeiro, it is necessary to prepare beforehand. This involves studying the cost of lodgings, transportation, and attractions. Search for offers and discounts on travel websites and social media groups. Additionally, attempt to go during the off-season, since rates tend to be cheaper. By preparing ahead, you might have a better understanding of how much money you need to spend for your vacation.

Establish a Daily Budget
After you have an estimate of the cost of your vacation, determine a daily budget for yourself. This will assist you in staying on budget and avoiding paying too much. Be sure to include lodgings, transportation, food, and attractions in your budget.

Stay in Budget-friendly Lodgings
Accommodations in Rio de Janeiro may be pricey, particularly if you opt to stay in a hotel. Instead, think about reserving a hostel room or renting an apartment. These solutions are frequently more budget-friendly and allow the ability to make your meals, saving you money on dining out.

Take Public Transportation
Rio de Janeiro has an extensive public transit system, including buses and metro. Taking public transit is significantly cheaper than using taxis or utilizing ride-sharing services. Consider obtaining a metro card, which may be used on both the metro and bus system.

Dine Like a Local
Dining out in Rio de Janeiro may be pricey, particularly in tourist districts. To save money, eat like a local. Search for street sellers serving traditional Brazilian cuisine or visit local markets to get fresh produce and ingredients. Additionally, try making your meals at your lodgings.

Take Advantage of Free Attractions
Rio de Janeiro features several free attractions, including the famed Copacabana and Ipanema beaches. You may also visit the Botanical Garden, the National Museum of Brazil, and the Rio de Janeiro Cathedral for free. Take advantage of these attractions to save money on entertainment.

Be Wary of Scammers
As any big tourist destination, Rio de Janeiro has its fair share of scammers. Be careful of persons attempting to sell you expensive trinkets, taxi drivers overcharging you, and pickpockets. Always use caution and pay attention to your surroundings.

Carry Cash
Although many establishments in Rio de Janeiro accept credit cards, it is still a smart idea to bring

cash. This is particularly important if you intend on visiting markets or street sellers, since they typically do not take credit cards. Be careful to put your cash in a safe area, such as a money belt or concealed pocket.

Budgeting and managing money in Rio de Janeiro needs careful preparation and common sense. By establishing a daily budget, staying in budget-friendly hotels, utilizing public transit, dining like a local, taking advantage of free attractions, being alert of scams, and carrying cash, you can enjoy everything that Rio de Janeiro has to offer without breaking the bank.

Language and Communication

Rio de Janeiro is a bustling city in Brazil that draws people from all over the globe. For tourists, learning the language and communication in Rio de Janeiro may enrich their experience and allow for better relationships with locals.

The official language of Brazil is Portuguese, and this is the major language spoken in Rio de Janeiro. Nonetheless, owing to the city's cosmopolitan background, many inhabitants speak many languages, including Spanish and English. In tourist districts and hotels, English is often spoken, but it is always a good idea to acquire a few basic phrases in Portuguese to aid with regular conversation.

In Rio de Janeiro, conversation is frequently energetic and expressive. Brazilians are recognized for their warm and welcoming disposition, and this is mirrored in their communication style. It is usual for natives to employ hand gestures and body language to reinforce their argument or communicate emotion. Tourists should not be astonished to see individuals embracing, kissing, or caressing one other during discussions, since this is a cultural norm in Brazil.

When addressing someone in Rio de Janeiro, it is necessary to use formal titles, particularly when meeting someone for the first time. For example, instead of using someone's first name, it is best to use "Senhor" or "Senhora" (Mr. or Mrs.) followed by their last name. In more casual circumstances, such as with friends or relatives, first names might be used.

In terms of written communication, Portuguese is the language used for government papers, street signs, and menus. Tourists should be prepared to encounter menus in Portuguese, however many eateries provide English translations as well. **Some fundamental Portuguese phrases to learn include:**

- Olá (Hi) (Hello)

- Obrigado (Thank you) (Thank you)

- Per favor (Please) (Please)

- Desculpe (Forgive me) (Excuse me)

- Sim (Yes) (Yes)

- Não (No) (No)

- Tchau (Goodbye) (Goodbye)

It is also crucial to note that Rio de Janeiro has its own distinct slang and accent, known as "carioca." This dialect might be difficult for non-native speakers to comprehend, but it contributes to the distinctive character of the city. **Some typical carioca expressions include:**

- Beleza? (How's it going?)

- Valeu! (Thanks!)

- Firmeza? (Is everything okay?)

- Tá ligado? (You know what I mean?)

- Maneiro! (Cool!)

Nevertheless, communication in Rio de Janeiro is friendly and expressive, and tourists may improve their experience by learning some basic Portuguese words and being receptive to the city's distinctive accent and communication style. With its magnificent beaches, rich culture, and friendly residents, Rio de Janeiro is a must-visit destination for every visitor.

Visa Requirements and Customs

If you are considering a vacation to Rio de Janeiro, it is crucial to know the visa requirements and customs restrictions before you arrive. **This is an outline of everything you need to know:**

Visa Requirements
Brazil has a visa policy that defines which nations need a visa to visit the country. Visitors from select countries are free from a visa needed for short visits, but most tourists will need a visa to enter Brazil.

To find out whether you need a visa for Brazil, you should check the Brazilian embassy or consulate in your own country or visit the Brazilian government's official visa website. The Brazilian government provides electronic visas for specific nations, which may be purchased online before going to Brazil.

Customs Regulations
When landing at Rio de Janeiro, you will need to go through customs clearance. Brazilian customs restrictions are comparable to those of other nations and ban certain things from being transported into the country. It is crucial to know what you can and

cannot carry into Brazil to prevent any complications at customs.

Some of the goods that are forbidden from being brought into Brazil include guns, explosives, and drugs. Also, there are limitations on the quantity of alcohol and cigarette items that you may carry into the nation.

Before traveling through customs control, you will need to fill out a declaration form that specifies all of the things that you are carrying into the nation. If you are carrying more than $10,000 USD or its equivalent in other currencies, you will need to disclose it to customs officers.

It is also crucial to understand that customs authorities in Brazil have the power to check your bags and valuables. If you are discovered to be carrying any banned things, they may be seized, and you might face fines or other consequences.

Also, it is necessary to be respectful to Brazilian culture and traditions. Dress modestly while visiting holy locations, and avoid wearing exposing apparel on the beach or in other public settings. Brazilians are also incredibly loving, so be prepared for hugs and kisses on the cheek when meeting new people.

Rio de Janeiro is a dynamic and interesting city that welcomes people from throughout the globe. By understanding the visa requirements and customs restrictions, you may have a safe and happy journey to this lovely city.

Itinerary Planning

Here's an itinerary to help you make the most of your stay in this great city:

Day 1: Explore Historic Rio

- Start your journey by experiencing the historic center of Rio.
- Begin your day with the famed Christ the Redeemer monument, one of the most prominent sites in Rio.
- Take a train journey to the summit of Corcovado Mountain, where the monument resides, and enjoy the panoramic views of the city.

- Next, proceed to the ancient area of Santa Teresa, where you can view some of Rio's most exquisite colonial buildings.
- Take a trip through the small, twisting lanes and visit the Chácara do Céu Museum, which includes a collection of Brazilian art.
- In the evening, travel to Lapa, one of Rio's liveliest areas, to enjoy the city's legendary nightlife. Grab a drink at one of the numerous bars and enjoy the live music and dancing.

Day 2: Beach Day

- Spend the second day of your vacation soaking up the sun on one of Rio's stunning beaches.
- Start your day at Ipanema Beach, one of the most renowned beaches in the world, where you may hire a chair and umbrella and relax on the sand.
- In the afternoon, travel to Copacabana Beach, another classic Rio site, and meander along the promenade.
- If you're feeling daring, try some of the water activities on offer, such as surfing or stand-up paddleboarding.

Day 3: Tijuca National Park

- On your third day in Rio, visit Tijuca National Park, the biggest urban forest in the world.
- Take a guided tour of the park and trek to the summit of Pedra Bonita, which gives beautiful views of the city and the coastline.
- In the afternoon, explore the Jardim Botânico, a stunning botanical park with over 8,000 plant varieties.
- Take a leisurely walk around the grounds and appreciate the unique flowers and plants.

Day 4: Sugarloaf Mountain

- Spend your final day in Rio touring Sugarloaf Mountain, another renowned sight in the city.
- Take a cable car to the top of the mountain and enjoy the beautiful views of Rio and the surrounding shoreline.
- In the afternoon, go to the Museum of Tomorrow, a futuristic museum that addresses

the difficulties confronting mankind in the 21st century. The museum features interactive displays that are both instructive and amusing.

This schedule will give you a taste of everything Rio de Janeiro has to offer, but there are many additional things to see and do in this great city. Don't be scared to explore and uncover some hidden treasures of your own!

Chapter 2

Top Attractions

Rio de Janeiro is one of the most famous and energetic cities in the world, situated in Brazil's southern region. Renowned for its magnificent beaches, colorful culture, and energetic nightlife, Rio de Janeiro has something to offer for everyone. It is a city that draws people from all over the globe, who come to enjoy the unique blend of natural beauty and urban activity.

In this guide, we will examine some of the greatest attractions in Rio de Janeiro that tourists should not miss, including historic sites, cultural hotspots, and activities that display the city's natural beauty. Whether you are a first-time visitor or a seasoned tourist, there is always something new to discover in Rio de Janeiro. So, pack your bags and get ready to discover the top attractions that make Rio de Janeiro a must-visit destination.

1. Christ the Redeemer Statue

The Christ the Redeemer Statue, also known as Cristo Redentor in Portuguese, is a world-renowned symbol situated in Rio de Janeiro, Brazil. This huge statue of Jesus Christ sits towering on top of Corcovado Mountain and is regarded as one of the most magnificent sites in the world. It is one of the major locations for travelers in Rio de Janeiro, bringing millions of people every year.

The statue is built of reinforced concrete and soapstone and stands at a height of 98 feet (30 meters) on top of a pedestal that is 26 feet (8 meters) tall, bringing the overall height of the monument to 124 feet (38 meters) (38 meters). The arms of the monument spread out 92 feet (28 meters), signifying Christ's embrace of the city and the globe.

Christ the Redeemer was erected between 1922 and 1931 and was conceived by Brazilian engineer Heitor da Silva Costa, with the aid of French artist Paul Landowski. The monument was created to honor the centenary of Brazil's independence and is a symbol of the country's strong Catholic faith. It is also a monument to the expertise and inventiveness of Brazilian architects and engineers, who erected the statue using locally produced materials.

Tourists to Rio de Janeiro travel from all over the globe to view the Christ the Redeemer Monument. The monument is placed on top of Corcovado Mountain in the Tijuca National Forest and may be visited by rail, van or automobile. The train trip up to the top of the mountain is a popular method to visit the monument and gives beautiful views of the city and the surrounding terrain. Tourists may also go up to the summit of the mountain, however this is a tough trip that should only be undertaken by experienced hikers.

After travelers reach the summit of the mountain, they are welcomed with the stunning sight of the Christ the Redeemer Monument. The monument is visible from practically every area of the city and is especially attractive at night when it is lit. Tourists may climb up the pedestal to have a closer look at the monument and to take in the panoramic views of the city below.

There are also guided tours offered that give visitors with a fuller knowledge of the history and importance of the monument. These tours provide an immersive experience, enabling guests to learn about the cultural and religious importance of the monument, as well as the architectural achievements necessary to erect it.

In addition to the monument itself, there are numerous additional attractions situated atop Corcovado Mountain that tourists may enjoy. They include restaurants, cafés, and gift stores that offer souvenirs and memorabilia relating to the monument. The Tijuca National Forest is also home to many other natural treasures, such as waterfalls and hiking routes, that tourists may explore.

The Christ the Redeemer Monument is a major attraction in Rio de Janeiro for travelers. This majestic monument is not just a symbol of Brazil's strong Catholic faith but also a tribute to the talent and ingenuity of Brazilian architects and engineers. People travel from all over the globe to visit the monument and to enjoy the spectacular views of the city and the surrounding region. Whether you are a history enthusiast, a nature lover, or just seeking a spectacular tourist experience, the Christ the

Redeemer Monument is an attraction that should not be missed.

2. Sugarloaf Mountain

Sugarloaf Mountain, known as Pão de Açúcar in Portuguese, is a notable sight in Rio de Janeiro, Brazil. It is a granite peak that rises 396 meters above the bay of Rio de Janeiro, affording breathtaking panoramic views of the city and its surrounding environs. This renowned mountain is one of the most popular tourist spots in Rio, drawing tourists from all over the globe.

History

The Sugarloaf Mountain has a rich history. It is estimated to have been produced about 600 million years ago. The peak was initially found by the Portuguese in 1502 when they landed in Brazil. It was termed "Pão de Açúcar" or "Sugarloaf" because of its similarity to the sugarloafs that were used to refine sugar during the colonial era.

In 1912, the first cable car was installed on the mountain, which transformed the way people could access the peak. Currently, Sugarloaf Mountain is one of the most prominent tourist destinations in Brazil, and its cable cars are a key lure for tourists.

Visiting Sugarloaf Mountain

Visiting Sugarloaf Mountain is an incredible experience. The mountain is situated in the Urca area, and tourists may reach the peak by boarding two cable cars. The first cable car carries guests to the top of Urca Hill, while the second cable car takes them to the peak of Sugarloaf Mountain. The voyage is a beautiful experience, as tourists are given to stunning views of the city and the port.

Once reaching the peak, guests may take a leisurely walk around the observation deck to enjoy the magnificent views of Rio de Janeiro. The observation deck gives a 360-degree view of the city, and visitors can see prominent sights such as the Christ the Redeemer monument, Copacabana Beach, and the Guanabara Bay. The vista is especially stunning after sunset, when the sky transforms into colors of orange, pink, and purple.

There are also a few restaurants and cafés at the peak, where guests may enjoy a meal or a drink while taking in the spectacular views. The souvenir stores offer a range of items, including T-shirts, keychains, and postcards.

Suggestions for Tourists

To make the most of your visit to Sugarloaf Mountain, **here are some recommendations to bear in mind:**

Purchase Your Tickets in Advance: The lineups for the cable car may become lengthy, particularly during high season. It is advisable to buy your tickets in advance to escape the lineups and save time.

Dress Comfortably: The weather at the peak might be very different from the weather at the bottom. It may be windy and colder, so dress in layers and wear comfortable shoes.

Bring a Camera: The views from Sugarloaf Peak are incredibly breathtaking, so make sure to bring a camera to preserve the moments.

Visit During Sunset: The sunset views from Sugarloaf Mountain are incredibly spectacular, and it is one of the greatest times to visit.

Be Aware of Your Possessions: Like with any tourist site, be mindful of your belongings and keep a watch on your valuables.

Sugarloaf Mountain is a prominent landmark in Rio de Janeiro that gives breathtaking views of the city and its surroundings. The climb to the top on the cable car is an amazing experience, and the panoramic views from the observation deck are truly spectacular. It is a must-visit place for anybody visiting Rio de Janeiro, and a fantastic opportunity to observe the city from a fresh perspective.

3. Copacabana Beach

Copacabana Beach is one of the most renowned and popular beaches in Rio de Janeiro, Brazil. It spans for approximately 4 kilometers and is situated in the southern portion of the city, between the districts of Copacabana and Leme. The beach is noted for its breathtaking surroundings, golden beaches, crystal-clear waves, and vibrant atmosphere. With its particular beauty, Copacabana Beach is a must-visit site for every visitor visiting Rio de Janeiro.

History and Culture
The history of Copacabana Beach can be traced back to the early 1900s when it was still a very tiny and underdeveloped beach. Yet, as the city expanded and more people started to migrate to Rio de Janeiro, the attractiveness of Copacabana Beach rose as well. Nowadays, the beach is a symbol of Brazilian culture and is recognized for its active nightlife, beach sports, and music scene. The beach has also played home to several cultural events, including the iconic New Year's Eve celebration, which draws millions of people each year.

Activities
There is no lack of stuff to do at Copacabana Beach. The beach provides a broad variety of water activities, including swimming, surfing, and beach volleyball. Guests may also hire a stand-up paddleboard, jet ski, or take a boat excursion to explore the shoreline. For those who prefer to remain on land, there are lots of alternatives for

beachfront entertainment, including live music, street performers, and carnival-like events.

One of the most popular pastimes at Copacabana Beach is just sitting on the beach and soaking up the sun. Guests may hire beach chairs and umbrellas or bring their own and spend a relaxed day by the sea. The beach is also home to various beachfront cafés and restaurants where tourists can enjoy a refreshing drink or a wonderful meal while taking in the gorgeous views.

Attractions
In addition to its magnificent beach, Copacabana also offers numerous additional things worth seeing. One of the most renowned is the Copacabana Palace Hotel, a magnificent hotel that has housed celebrities and international leaders for over 100 years. The hotel's exquisite design and spectacular ocean views make it a popular place for travelers to come and snap photographs.

Another famous site is the Forte de Copacabana, a medieval military fort that overlooks the beach. Visitors may explore the fort and learn about its significance in Brazilian history, as well as take in the spectacular views of the coastline.

Moreover, there are numerous additional sites and monuments in the region, including the Copacabana Boardwalk, which is bordered with palm trees and contains various booths offering food and beverages.

Safety and Security
While Copacabana Beach is a major tourist attraction, it is vital to understand that the region may also be prone to crime. Visitors should take care to keep themselves and their things secure, such as avoiding carrying significant quantities of cash or valuables, and staying in well-lit places at night. It is also vital to be careful of pickpockets and street merchants who may attempt to sell counterfeit items or defraud visitors.

Nevertheless, Copacabana Beach is a prominent tourist attraction in Rio de Janeiro for travelers wishing to experience the lively culture and natural beauty of Brazil. With its breathtaking environment, extensive selection of activities, and cultural attractions, there is something for everyone to enjoy at this legendary beach.

4. Ipanema Beach

Ipanema Beach is one of the most renowned beaches in the world, situated in the upmarket area of Ipanema in Rio de Janeiro, Brazil. With its golden dunes, crystal-clear seas, and magnificent surroundings, it is a major tourist attraction that draws millions of people every year.

One of the biggest charms of Ipanema Beach is its natural beauty. The beach is bordered by lush green hills, which create a lovely background to the turquoise seas of the Atlantic Ocean. The sand is smooth and powdery, and continues for 2.5 kilometers down the shore. Tourists may enjoy a range of sports, such as swimming, surfing, sunbathing, and beach volleyball.

In addition to its natural beauty, Ipanema Beach is also noted for its colorful environment. The beach is dotted with bars, restaurants, and cafés, where tourists may taste some of the local food and beverages. There are also numerous street sellers offering a selection of souvenirs and handicrafts, making it a fantastic spot to pick up some keepsakes of your stay.

One of the most prominent views at Ipanema Beach is the two mountains known as Dois Irmãos (Two Brothers), which are visible from the beach. The mountains are a popular site for hikers, who may trek to the peak for stunning views of the beach and the surrounding environment.

Ipanema Beach is also noted for its bustling nightlife. There are several pubs and nightclubs in the region, which draw both residents and visitors alike. Guests may enjoy live music, dance the night away, or just sit back and relax with a drink in hand.

Safety is always a worry while traveling, but tourists can rest assured that Ipanema Beach is typically regarded as a safe site to visit. There is a police station situated on the beach, and there are also lifeguards on duty throughout the day. But, it is always a good idea to take measures and keep a watch on your possessions, particularly while in busy locations.

Ultimately, Ipanema Beach is a must-visit place for anybody visiting Rio de Janeiro. Its natural beauty, vibrant ambiance, and choice of activities make it a favorite tourist site that is guaranteed to leave tourists with great experiences.

5. The Selaron Steps

The Selaron Steps, commonly known as Escadaria Selarón or the "Selaron Staircase," is one of the main tourist locations in Rio de Janeiro. This brilliant and colorful staircase, situated in the bohemian area of Lapa, is a must-visit location for travelers visiting Rio de Janeiro.

The Selaron Steps were designed by Chilean artist Jorge Selaron, who came to Rio de Janeiro in the early 1980s. Selaron started the project in 1990 as a method to revive the decaying stairwell that led up to his house. He began by laying some tiles on the stairs, and as he continued to work on it, the project blossomed into a big creative undertaking. Selaron spent over 20 years renovating the stairs into an incredible piece of art, covering the 215 steps with over 2000 tiles acquired from all around the globe.

The multicolored tiles that cover the Selaron Steps originate from over 60 different nations, including Brazil, Portugal, France, and Argentina. The tiles are a variety of colors, patterns, and textures, producing a unique and aesthetically spectacular masterpiece. Selaron employed his own creative approach to create a coherent aesthetic, and the outcome is a dazzling display of color and design.

In addition to the tiles, Selaron also put several paintings, sculptures, and other items of art on the staircase. The staircase is a real expression of Selaron's varied style, and each step bears a narrative and a piece of his life's work.

The Selaron Steps have become a renowned tourist spot in Rio de Janeiro, drawing tourists from all over the globe. The staircase has been featured in several films, music videos, and documentaries. It has also been visited by several celebrities, including Snoop Dogg, Madonna, and Jackie Chan.

Visitors to the Selaron Steps may take in the grandeur of the stairs and explore the area of Lapa. Lapa is noted for its bustling nightlife, samba music, and street art. Visitors may eat the local food, enjoy the music, and take in the vivid murals and street art that grace the walls of the area.

The Selaron Steps are readily accessible by public transit or cab. They are available to the public 24 hours a day, seven days a week, and there is no entry cost. Visitors are urged to take their time and admire the beauty of the staircase and the art that covers it.

The Selaron Steps is a prominent tourist spot in Rio de Janeiro that provides a distinctive and vivid experience for tourists. The staircase is a monument to the brilliance and passion of its builder, Jorge Selaron, and is a must-visit destination for anybody visiting Rio de Janeiro.

6. The Botanical Garden

One of the biggest tourist locations in Rio de Janeiro is the Botanical Garden, better known as the Jardim Botânico.

The Botanical Garden is a magnificent green paradise situated in the middle of the city, encompassing an area of 137 hectares. It was created in 1808 by Prince Regent Dom João VI, and now it is one of the most significant botanical research institutes in Brazil, containing approximately 8,000 varieties of plants, including endangered and uncommon species.

Visitors to the Botanical Garden may enjoy a calm respite from the rush and bustle of the city and immerse themselves in the beauty of nature. The park offers a diverse assortment of flora, including gigantic Amazonian water lilies, towering palm trees, and exotic orchids. The garden is also home to a variety of species, including monkeys, toucans, and sloths, making it an ideal destination for nature enthusiasts and birdwatchers.

One of the most notable features of the Botanical Garden is the Avenue of Royal Palms, which comprises over 100 large palm trees set in a straight line that leads visitors to the main entrance of the park. This amazing sight is great for capturing photographs and appreciating the beauty of nature.

Another feature of the Botanical Garden is the greenhouse, which holds a varied array of tropical plants and flowers from all over the globe. Within the greenhouse, visitors may discover rare varieties of orchids, bromeliads, and other exotic plants.

The Botanical Garden also provides guided tours, which are a fantastic opportunity to learn about the history and ecology of the garden. The guides are informed and enthusiastic about the flora and creatures in the garden and are always eager to answer questions.

In addition to its natural beauty, the Botanical Garden is also a cultural and historical treasure. The garden was formerly the location of the Imperial Family's summer retreat, and now tourists may explore the remains of the palace and its surrounding gardens.

The Botanical Garden is open every day of the year, and entry is reasonable. It is readily accessible by public transit, and there are also plenty of parking places available for those who want to drive. Guests are urged to bring comfortable shoes, sunscreen, and a hat to protect themselves from the sun.

The Botanical Garden is a must-see location for anybody visiting Rio de Janeiro. It is a fantastic spot to rest, unwind, and immerse oneself in the beauty of nature. Whether you are a nature lover, a history enthusiast, or just searching for a calm respite from the city, the Botanical Garden is a fantastic option.

7. The Maracana Stadium

The Maracana Stadium is one of the main tourist locations in Rio de Janeiro, Brazil. It is a vast sports stadium that has held various events, including the 1950 World Cup final and the 2016 Olympic Games opening ceremony.

Guests may take a guided tour of the stadium, which includes a visit to the museum and a chance to view the locker rooms, the press room, and the field. The tour also offers guests an understanding of the stadium's history and its relevance to Brazilian sports culture.

For soccer enthusiasts, witnessing a game at the Maracana Stadium is an amazing experience. The stadium has a seating capacity of nearly 78,000, and the atmosphere is electrifying during games. The local soccer clubs Flamengo and Fluminense usually play matches at the stadium, and tickets may be bought online or via local merchants.

Ultimately, the Maracana Stadium is a must-visit venue for sports enthusiasts and everyone interested in Brazilian culture. With its rich history and amazing dimensions, it gives a unique view into the world of Brazilian sports and culture.

8. The Rio Carnival

The Rio Carnival is one of the world's most renowned and beautiful festivities, bringing millions of tourists to Rio de Janeiro every year. This bright and exuberant celebration takes place over four days, generally in February or early March, and is celebrated with parades, parties, and samba dance across the city.

The Carnival is strongly ingrained in Brazilian culture and customs, and its beginnings may be traced back to the 18th century. Nowadays, the festival is a big cultural event that draws people from all over the globe who come to experience the unique energy and excitement of this celebration.

During the Rio Carnival, visitors may enjoy a multitude of events and activities, from the sumptuous parades showcasing ornate floats and colorful costumes, to street parties where residents and tourists alike dance to the rhythm of samba music. Several of the city's prominent attractions, like the famed Christ the Redeemer statue and Sugarloaf Mountain, are also popular locations for travelers during the Carnival.

Although the Rio Carnival is absolutely a must-see event, tourists should be advised that the celebration may be extremely overwhelming and congested, with high demand for lodging and tickets. Nonetheless, with good planning and preparation, attending the Rio Carnival may be a genuinely spectacular and once-in-a-lifetime event.

Chapter 3

Where to Stay

Overview of Rio de Janeiro's Neighborhoods

Rio de Janeiro is a bustling and diversified city, with a broad variety of districts that give tourists distinct experiences. **This is a quick description of some of the most popular neighborhoods:**

Copacabana: Renowned for its beautiful beach, Copacabana is a lively area with a mix of hotels, restaurants, clubs, and stores. It's a terrific area to enjoy the excitement of Rio and soak up the sun.

Ipanema: Located south of Copacabana, Ipanema is another renowned beach district with a more upmarket air. It's home to high-end boutiques and restaurants, as well as the renowned "Girl from Ipanema" song.

Lapa: This ancient area is renowned for its vibrant nightlife and samba clubs. It's a terrific venue to explore the music and dancing culture of Rio.

Santa Teresa: A bohemian district set on a hill, Santa Teresa provides tourists a look into Rio's creative and cultural milieu. It's home to quaint cafés, art galleries, and breathtaking views over the city.

Flamengo: A more residential district, Flamengo is home to a big park and various institutions, including the famed Museum of Modern Art. It's a terrific spot to escape the hustle and bustle of the city and enjoy some green space.

Leblon: Situated near the southern end of Ipanema, Leblon is another posh district featuring high-end stores and restaurants. It's recognized for its stunning coastline and views of the Morro Dois Irmãos peak.

No matter the district you choose to visit, Rio de Janeiro is guaranteed to give a unique and remarkable experience.

Accommodation Options

Rio de Janeiro is one of the most popular locations in South America, drawing people from all across the globe with its magnificent beaches, lively culture, and thrilling nightlife. As such, there are lots of lodging alternatives accessible for travelers, ranging from luxury hotels to budget-friendly hostels.

Hotels: Rio de Janeiro offers a large choice of hotels to choose from, catering to all budgets and interests. The most opulent hotels are situated in the wealthy areas of Copacabana, Ipanema, and Leblon, where tourists can expect to discover top-notch facilities, such as infinity pools, rooftop bars, and seaside views. Some of the greatest luxury hotels in Rio de Janeiro are the Belmond Copacabana Palace, the Grand Hyatt Rio de Janeiro, and the Sofitel Rio de Janeiro Ipanema.

For those on a tighter budget, there are lots of mid-range hotels and boutique rooms dispersed across the city. Several of these businesses provide pleasant accommodations, great service, and handy locations for relatively inexpensive prices. Some suggested mid-range hotels in Rio de Janeiro are the Hotel Atlântico Copacabana, the Arena Leme Hotel, and the Windsor Asturias Hotel.

Hostels: Hostels are a popular housing choice for backpackers and budget visitors, and Rio de Janeiro offers some of the greatest hostels in South America. Hostels in Rio de Janeiro provide dormitory-style lodging with shared toilets, community kitchens, and common spaces for socializing. Several hostels also offer private rooms with ensuite bathrooms for individuals who desire more solitude.

One of the nicest hostels in Rio de Janeiro is the Mango Tree Hostel, situated in the bohemian area of Santa Teresa. This hostel provides a casual environment, great views of the city, and many services, including a bar, a pool, and complimentary breakfast. Some suggested hostels in Rio de Janeiro include the Discovery Hostel, the Lemon Spirit Hostel, and the El Misti Hostel.

Airbnb: Airbnb is a popular alternative to conventional hotels and hostels in Rio de Janeiro, providing guests the option to stay in local areas and experience the city like a local. Rio de Janeiro offers lots of Airbnb alternatives to select from, ranging from single rooms in local homes to complete flats and mansions.

Some of the greatest districts to stay in while reserving an Airbnb in Rio de Janeiro are Copacabana, Ipanema, and Santa Teresa. These locations give convenient access to the city's major attractions, superb food choices, and lots of cultural events. When considering an Airbnb in Rio de Janeiro, make careful to check reviews and connect with the owner before booking to guarantee a pleasant and safe stay.

Vacation Rentals: Vacation rentals are another popular lodging choice in Rio de Janeiro, particularly for families or bigger groups visiting together. Vacation homes may provide more room, privacy, and amenities than standard hotels or hostels, making them a perfect alternative for individuals searching for a home away from home.

One of the top vacation rental firms in Rio de Janeiro is Casa Cool Beans, which provides a range of boutique villas in the fashionable district of Santa Teresa. These houses feature distinctive designs, private pools, and breathtaking views of the city. Some suggested vacation rental firms in Rio de Janeiro include Rio Exclusive, Villa Rio, and Wimdu.

Rio de Janeiro provides a broad selection of hotel alternatives to meet all budgets and interests. Whether you're searching for a luxury hotel or a budget-friendly hostel, there's something for everyone in this dynamic city. While picking lodging in Rio de Janeiro, be sure to consider your budget, chosen location, and desired facilities to locate the best place to stay during your vacation.

Tips for Finding the Best Deals

Rio de Janeiro is a popular tourist destination, and getting the best discounts for lodgings may be tough. **Here are some recommendations to assist travelers locate the greatest bargains for lodgings in Rio de Janeiro:**

Book in Advance: Booking early might help you receive the greatest rates on lodgings. Several hotels and hostels offer discounts for early reservations.

Compare Pricing: It is crucial to compare costs from several sources, including hotel booking websites, travel agencies, and direct booking with the hotel. This will help you find the greatest prices.

Select the Appropriate Location: The location of your hotel might affect the pricing. Try staying in less popular places or in communities that are well-connected to public transit.

Look for Deals and Discounts: Hotels and hostels regularly offer promotions and discounts, particularly during low season or vacations. Be sure to check their websites or social media accounts for offers.

Explore Alternate Accommodations: Airbnb, hostels, and homestays might be cheaper alternatives to hotels. They may also give a more real experience of the place.

Utilize Loyalty Programs: Several hotel chains have loyalty programs that give advantages and discounts for repeat clients. Join up for these programs if you intend to visit Rio de Janeiro often.

By following these recommendations, tourists may locate the finest prices on hotels in Rio de Janeiro, saving money while still enjoying everything that this beautiful city has to offer.

Chapter 4

Food and Drink

Rio de Janeiro, a city that is recognized for its colorful culture, magnificent beaches, and wonderful cuisine. Rio's food is a combination of elements from Portuguese, African, and indigenous cultures, resulting in a unique gastronomic experience.

In this busy metropolis, you will find everything from street food sellers providing traditional Brazilian snacks to high-end restaurants giving innovative interpretations on classic foods.
Whether you're a foodie or simply searching for some good cuisine, Rio de Janeiro offers something for everyone.

In this guide, we'll examine some of the must-try foods and beverages in Rio, as well as where to locate them. So be ready to relish in the delicacies of Rio de Janeiro!

Brazilian Cuisine and Specialties

Brazilian food is a tasty and unique combination of Portuguese, African, and indigenous tastes and customs. It varies considerably throughout various parts of the nation, and Rio de Janeiro has its own particular characteristics.

One of the most renowned foods in Rio de Janeiro is feijoada, a robust stew composed with black beans, different cuts of pig, beef, and sausage. It's often served with rice, farofa (toasted manioc flour), and sautéed collard greens. Other popular foods in Rio include:
- Churrasco (grilled meats),
- Moqueca (a fish stew), and
- Coxinha (a deep-fried pastry filled with shredded chicken)

Seafood is also a large element of Rio's cuisine, considering the city is situated on the coast. Visitors should sample the grilled shrimp, squid, and octopus dishes, as well as the famed bolinhos do bacalhau (codfish fritters).

For dessert, brigadeiro is a must-try. It's a chocolate truffle prepared with condensed milk and cocoa powder, rolled in chocolate sprinkles. Another typical sweet delicacy is quindim, a coconut and egg yolk cake.

In addition to the cuisine, tourists visiting Rio should also experience the city's distinctive drink, the caipirinha. Composed with cachaça (a sugar cane liquor), lime, and sugar, it's a pleasant and strong drink.

Overall, Rio de Janeiro offers a broad and tasty cuisine that blends a variety of ethnic influences. Visitors should taste the local dishes and discover the city's dynamic culinary scene.

Top Restaurants and Bars in Rio de Janeiro

Rio de Janeiro is a bustling city that offers a multitude of food and drinking alternatives for guests. These are some top restaurants and bars to check out:

Aprazível: This restaurant is situated in the hilly Santa Teresa district and offers wonderful views of the city. They specialize in Brazilian cuisine, using organic products acquired from their own farm.

Garota de Ipanema: Situated in the iconic Ipanema area, this tavern and restaurant is famous for being the basis for the popular bossa nova song of the same name. They serve traditional Brazilian meals and have a lively ambiance.

Bar do Mineiro: This laid-back pub in Santa Teresa is a favorite among locals and travelers alike. They serve wonderful caipirinhas and traditional Brazilian foods such as feijoada.

Mee: This contemporary Asian restaurant is located in the Belmond Copacabana Palace hotel and offers a unique combination of Japanese, Thai, and Chinese food.

Bar Astor: Located on the oceanfront of Ipanema, this bar is the perfect site to enjoy a nice drink and watch the sunset. They provide a choice of drinks, beers, and wines, as well as wonderful bar food.

Zuka: This restaurant in Leblon provides a selection of international food with a Brazilian flair. They feature a small, intimate ambiance and an excellent wine list.

Cervantes: This no-frills sandwich store in Copacabana is a must-visit for anyone searching for a great and economical dinner. These sandwiches are packed with grilled meats and topped with melted cheese.

These are just a few of the many amazing restaurants and pubs that Rio de Janeiro has to offer. Whether you're seeking traditional Brazilian delicacies or foreign food, there is something for everyone in this dynamic city.

Street Food and Snacks

Rio de Janeiro is a city noted for its street cuisine and snacks, which provide tourists a delightful sample of Brazil's culinary culture. These are some of the most popular street cuisine and snacks to sample in Rio de Janeiro:

Coxinha: A deep-fried snack prepared with shredded chicken and dough fashioned into a teardrop, like a chicken drumstick. It's commonly served with spicy sauce.

Pastel: A pastry filled with different items like cheese, ground beef, or vegetables, then deep-fried till crispy.

Açaí: A smoothie-like drink created from the superfood berry Açaí, combined with banana, oats, and other fruits.

Tapioca: A gluten-free pancake made from cassava flour, filled with cheese, coconut, or meat.

Pão de Queijo: Little cheese bread balls made with cassava flour and cheese.

Brigadeiro: A delicious chocolate truffle made with condensed milk and cocoa powder.

Churros: Deep-fried dough pastry wrapped in sugar and cinnamon, frequently filled with dulce de leche.

Empada: Little pies filled with chicken, cheese, or shrimp, similar to quiche.

These street meals and snacks may be obtained in various areas throughout Rio de Janeiro, including street sellers, markets, and cafés. They're inexpensive and give a fast, tasty sample of Brazil's distinct tastes. But, like with any street food, it's necessary to exercise care and find reliable sellers to prevent food poisoning or other health dangers.

Vegetarian and Vegan Options

Rio de Janeiro, Brazil is a bustling and varied city that provides a range of vegetarian and vegan culinary alternatives for travelers. Whether you're a staunch vegan, a vegetarian, or just trying to minimize your meat diet, Rio de Janeiro offers lots of alternatives to select from.

One of the most popular vegetarian and vegan restaurants in Rio de Janeiro is Naturalie Bistro. Situated in the Botafogo area, this restaurant serves a choice of excellent vegetarian and vegan cuisine, including salads, sandwiches, and pasta dishes, as well as a selection of smoothies and juices.

Another wonderful alternative is Vegana Chácara, which provides an entirely vegan cuisine with items including burgers, falafel, and vegan cheese. Situated in the Santa Teresa district, this quaint location is excellent for a relaxed lunch or supper.

If you're searching for a more upmarket eating experience, Refeitório Orgânico is an excellent alternative. This restaurant, situated in the Jardim Botânico district, provides a fresh, vegetarian cuisine that varies often. Their meals are produced using fresh, organic ingredients and are tastefully presented.

For a fast and excellent bite, guests may stop at Bibi Sucos. This network of juice bars provides a range of vegetarian and vegan alternatives, including acai bowls, sandwiches, and fresh fruit smoothies.

Rio de Janeiro also boasts many traditional Brazilian eateries that provide vegetarian and vegan alternatives. For example, Casa de Feijoada, a restaurant specialized in Brazil's national food, provides a vegetarian version of feijoada cooked with tofu instead of beef. Also, most churrascarias (Brazilian steakhouses) feature a salad bar with vegetarian and vegan alternatives.

Rio de Janeiro is a city that provides lots of vegetarian and vegan culinary alternatives for guests. Whether you're searching for a fast snack or a gourmet supper, there are plenty of eateries to pick from that cater to a plant-based diet.

Chapter 5

Nightlife and Entertainment

Rio de Janeiro, usually known as Rio, is a bustling and diversified city that provides an amazing nightlife and entertainment scene for tourists. Being one of the most popular tourist attractions in Brazil, Rio is recognized for its beautiful beaches, boisterous street celebrations, and frenetic samba music.

From dusk to daybreak, the city comes alive with a range of entertainment choices, including dance clubs, live music venues, and pubs. Visitors may enjoy the city's rich culture and festive atmosphere by touring the local neighborhoods and partaking in the festivities. With so much to see and do, Rio de Janeiro is a must-visit location for those seeking an exciting nightlife and entertainment experience.

Clubs, Bars, and Music Venues

Rio de Janeiro is one of the most dynamic cities in the world, with a robust nightlife culture. Whether you're wanting to dance the night away at a club, have a few drinks at a bar, or watch some live music at a venue, Rio offers something for everyone. **Here's a quick summary of some of the greatest clubs, pubs, and music venues in Rio de Janeiro for visitors:**

Clubbing

The Week: One of the largest and most popular gay clubs in Rio de Janeiro, noted for its great sound system and energetic atmosphere.

Casa da Matriz: A famous club in the Botafogo district, showcasing indie and rock music and a mixed population.

Fosfobox: A club in Copacabana that caters to a younger population, featuring electronic music and a relaxing ambiance.

Bars

Bar do Mineiro: A classic Brazilian bar in Santa Teresa, famed for its caipirinhas and great bar cuisine.

Jobi: A famous pub in Ipanema, selling cool drinks and typical Brazilian delicacies like bolinhos de bacalhau (cod fritters).

Academy do Cachaça: A bar in Leblon that specializes in cachaça, Brazil's national spirit, and provides a broad choice of drinks crafted with this delectable liquor.

Music venues

Circo Voador: An iconic music venue in Lapa, offering live concerts and DJ performances from a broad spectrum of performers.

Audio Rebel: A tiny venue in Botafogo, recognized for its varied music programming and intimate environment.

Theatro Municipal: One of the most prominent cultural institutions in Rio de Janeiro, providing classical music events and operas in a gorgeous art deco edifice.

No matter what type of nightlife experience you're searching for, Rio de Janeiro has plenty to offer. But be sure to follow the standard precautions while going out at night, such as avoiding carrying too much cash or valuables and being mindful of your surroundings.

Live Music and Performances

Rio de Janeiro is a bustling city with a rich tradition of live music and shows that draw people from all over the globe. **These are some of the top alternatives for witnessing live music in Rio:**

Samba: Rio de Janeiro is famed for its samba music and dancing. The finest spot to enjoy samba is in the Lapa district, which is home to several restaurants and clubs that specialize in live samba performances.

Bossa Nova: Another prominent kind of music that developed in Rio de Janeiro is bossa nova. Guests may enjoy live bossa nova performances at numerous places across the city, including jazz clubs, pubs, and restaurants.

Street Performances: Rio de Janeiro is also renowned for its street performers who can be seen all throughout the city, particularly in tourist districts like Copacabana and Ipanema. These artists display a broad variety of abilities, including music, dance, and acrobatics.

Theatro Municipal: The Theatro Municipal is a historic theater in the city of Rio de Janeiro that stages a range of live acts, including opera, ballet, and classical music concerts.

Rio Scenarium: This renowned nightclub in Lapa is noted for its vibrant ambiance and live music performances, including a mix of samba, jazz, and other Brazilian music forms.

Nevertheless, Rio de Janeiro provides a varied choice of live music and performance opportunities for tourists to enjoy. Whether you're like samba, bossa nova, or simply want to experience the city's colorful culture, there's something for everyone in Rio.

Cultural Events and Festivals

Rio de Janeiro is one of the most dynamic and culturally rich cities in the world, noted for its colorful festivals and events that bring people from all over the globe. These are some of the most popular cultural events and festivals in Rio de Janeiro that tourists should check out:

Carnival - This is certainly the greatest and most renowned celebration in Rio de Janeiro, occurring annually in February or March. The city comes alive with colorful parades, samba dancers, and street festivities that stretch for several days.

New Year's Eve - Held on the famed Copacabana Beach, this event is one of the biggest New Year's Eve parties in the world. The night is packed with fireworks, music, and celebrations, making it a unique experience.

Rio de Janeiro International Film Festival - Held in October, this festival highlights some of the top worldwide films and draws cinema aficionados from all over the globe.

Rock in Rio - This music event is held every two years and contains some of the greatest names in music, including worldwide musicians. The event lasts for many days and is a must-visit for music aficionados.

Festa Junina - This event honors the traditional Brazilian feast of Saint John the Baptist and is celebrated in June. Guests may enjoy traditional cuisine, music, and dances, making it a terrific opportunity to explore Brazilian culture.

Rio de Janeiro provides a diverse cultural experience with its various festivals and events, each presenting a unique peek into the city's colorful culture.

Chapter 6

Outdoor Activities

One of the finest ways to appreciate the beauty of Rio is via its varied outdoor activities. From hiking to surfing, there are lots of possibilities for tourists to explore and enjoy the city's natural surroundings.

Rio de Janeiro has a great blend of tropical temperature, majestic mountain ranges, and crystal blue waterways. Whether you are a thrill-seeker, a nature lover, or just searching for a pleasant outdoor excursion, Rio de Janeiro offers something for everyone. So be ready to see the finest of Rio's outdoors and immerse yourself in its natural beauty.

Hiking and Nature Walks

Rio de Janeiro is home to various natural parks and reserves, allowing tourists abundant chances for hiking and nature walks. One of the most popular hiking sites in the city is Tijuca National Park, the biggest urban forest in the world. Here, tourists may explore the lush foliage and spectacular waterfalls of the Atlantic rainforest, as well as view a variety of animal species such as monkeys, sloths, and rare birds.

Another famous hiking site is Pedra da Gávea, one of the highest mountains in Rio de Janeiro, affording stunning panoramic views of the city and the ocean. The trek to the summit is tough, but well worth the effort for the spectacular views. Other famous hiking spots are the Sugarloaf Mountain and Corcovado Mountain, which gives breathtaking views of the famed Christ the Redeemer monument.

Surfing and Beach Sports

Rio de Janeiro is home to some of the most gorgeous beaches in the world, therefore it's no wonder that surfing and beach sports are popular hobbies here. Some of the greatest beaches for surfing are Arpoador, Beach do Recreio, and Barra da Tijuca. Tourists may rent surfboards and receive lessons from skilled instructors to experience the excitement of catching a wave.

In addition to surfing, tourists may also enjoy a range of other beach activities such as beach volleyball, soccer, and paddleboarding. The beaches of Rio de Janeiro are also fantastic locations to relax and soak up the sun, with lots of vendors providing delicious coconut water and snacks.

Hang Gliding and Paragliding

For the more daring tourists, hang gliding and paragliding provide a thrilling opportunity to enjoy the breathtaking landscapes of Rio de Janeiro. Tourists may take off from the hills around the city and fly over the famed beaches and mountains, with stunning views of the city and the ocean.

Hang gliding and paragliding trips are provided with trained instructors who give all the required equipment and safety training. It's an incredible event that will leave guests with memories that last a lifetime.

Sailing and Boating

Rio de Janeiro is also an excellent location for sailing and boating aficionados, with its stunning shoreline and tranquil seas. Tourists may hire a sailboat or motorboat and explore the different beaches and islands near the city, including Ilha Grande and Angra dos Reis.

For a unique sailing experience, guests may also join a sunset cruise or a catamaran tour of the Guanabara Bay, where they can enjoy breathtaking views of the city skyline and renowned sights such as Sugarloaf Mountain and Christ the Redeemer.

Day Trips & Excursions

Finally, travelers to Rio de Janeiro may also take advantage of the city's closeness to other gorgeous places in Brazil. Some popular day outings and excursions include seeing the historical town of Paraty, the spectacular waterfalls of the Serra dos Órgãos National Park, and the gorgeous beaches of Búzios.

Some popular excursions include visiting the ancient town of Petrópolis, the old summer house of the Brazilian monarchs, and taking a jeep trip of the Tijuca National Park, where tourists may explore the jungle and view the Christ the Redeemer monument.

Chapter 7

Shopping

One of the main activities for visitors is shopping, since Rio de Janeiro is home to various shopping districts, malls, and marketplaces providing a broad selection of things at varied costs. From high-end luxury brands to local handicrafts, there is something for every shopper in Rio de Janeiro.

Shopping in Rio de Janeiro might be intimidating for first-time tourists, since the city is big and the retail alternatives are many. In this guide, I will present you with all the critical information you need to know to make the most of your shopping experience in Rio de Janeiro.

Local Markets and Street Vendors

Local markets and street sellers are a mainstay of Rio de Janeiro, where tourists can purchase anything from fresh vegetables and traditional delicacies to handcrafted crafts and unusual gifts. One of the most popular markets in the city is the Feira Hippie de

Ipanema, situated in the middle of Ipanema, one of the city's most wealthy areas. The market takes place every Sunday and contains a broad selection of handcrafted products, apparel, jewelry, and artwork, as well as street performers and live music.

Another famous market is the Feira de São Cristóvão, popularly known as the Feira Nordestina, which specialized in items and cuisines from Brazil's northeast area. Visitors may try traditional meals like tapioca, carne de sol, and feijoada, and peruse booths offering local crafts, apparel, and souvenirs. The market is open every day and is a terrific location to discover the culture and customs of Brazil's northeast.

For those searching for a more genuine and off-the-beaten-path experience, the Feira do Lavradio is a monthly antique and vintage market held in Rio's old downtown neighborhood. The market contains a range of antique apparel, furniture, literature, and artwork, as well as live music and food sellers. It's a terrific spot to study the city's history and uncover unique items.

Shopping Malls and Department Stores

Rio de Janeiro is home to various sophisticated shopping malls and department shops, where tourists may discover a broad choice of local and worldwide brands. One of the most popular malls is the Barra Shopping, situated in the Barra da Tijuca district. The mall has over 700 retailers, including major worldwide brands like Zara, H&M, and Apple, as well as indigenous Brazilian companies like Osklen and Havaianas.

Another prominent mall is the Rio Sul Shopping Center, situated in the Botafogo area, which contains over 400 retailers, a movie theater, and various eateries. The mall is an excellent area to buy for apparel, accessories, and technology, and also contains a range of Brazilian brands and designers.

For visitors searching for a more affluent shopping experience, the Fashion Mall in the São Conrado district is home to various high-end luxury retailers including Louis Vuitton, Prada, and Gucci, as well as expensive restaurants and cafés.

Souvenirs and Gifts

When it comes to souvenirs and presents, Rio de Janeiro has no lack of distinctive and unforgettable possibilities. One favorite souvenir is the canga, a bright and multifunctional beach towel that can also be worn as a scarf or wrap. Tourists may find cangas in local markets and beach sellers across the city.

Another popular present is the Havaianas flip-flop, a Brazilian company noted for its colorful and comfy styles. Tourists may find Havaianas in most shopping malls and department shops in Rio.

For those searching for a more traditional and genuine present, the Casa do Artesanato in the Lapa district is a terrific destination to purchase handcrafted crafts and souvenirs produced by local craftsmen. The shop provides a range of traditional Brazilian artifacts including wooden carvings, pottery, and woven baskets, as well as apparel and accessories created from natural materials like leather and cotton.

Rio de Janeiro provides tourists with a broad and fascinating shopping experience.

Chapter 8

Transportation

When it comes to moving about in Rio de Janeiro, there are various transit alternatives accessible to tourists. From cabs and buses to the famed cable cars and bicycles, Rio's transportation system has something for everyone. In this guide, I will give you an overview of the many transportation alternatives in Rio de Janeiro, along with some recommendations on how to traverse the city like a local. Whether you're here for business or pleasure, we hope this guide will help you make the most of your stay in Rio de Janeiro.

Getting to and From Rio de Janeiro

Rio de Janeiro has two airports, Galeão International Airport (GIG) and Santos Dumont Airport (SDU) (SDU). Galeão International Airport is the principal international airport, and it is situated approximately 20 kilometers north of the city center. Santos Dumont Airport is a domestic airport situated in the city core, near to the major tourist attractions. Tourists may easily travel to and from both airports via taxi, ride-sharing services or public transit.

The best method to travel to Rio de Janeiro from other regions of Brazil is via bus. The city features a big bus station, Rodoviária Novo Rio, which is situated in the city center and provides services to various cities in Brazil.

Traveling About the City via Public Transport

Rio de Janeiro offers a dependable and economical public transit system that includes buses, metro, and trains. The metro system is the quickest method to move about the city, particularly during peak hours when the roads might be crowded. The metro has two lines that cover the key tourist destinations, and the trains operate from 5 am to midnight.

Rio also has an enormous bus network that spans the whole city, however it may be tricky for outsiders to utilize. Tourists should plan their journeys in advance and be careful of the bus stations since they are not always properly indicated. The buses operate from 5 am to midnight, and the ticket may be paid with cash or the RioCard, a rechargeable card that can be used on both buses and metro.

Taxis and ride-sharing services

Taxis are a simple and safe method to move about Rio de Janeiro, and they are accessible 24/7. Taxis in Rio may be recognised by their yellow hue, and they utilize a meter to compute the rate. Tourists should be warned that taxis in Rio may be pricey, and it's vital to negotiate the rate before getting in the vehicle. Ride-sharing services such as Uber and Cabify are also accessible in Rio de Janeiro and are frequently cheaper than taxis.

Hiring a Vehicle or Bike

Renting a car in Rio de Janeiro is not suggested for tourists, since the traffic in the city may be hectic, and parking can be tough to locate. Nonetheless, those who prefer to hire a vehicle may do so at the airport or in the city center. Tourists may also hire bikes in Rio, and there are various bike rental firms available. Bicycling is a fantastic way to see the city, particularly along the seashore, and there are dedicated bike lanes in several spots.

In conclusion, tourists visiting Rio de Janeiro have various mobility alternatives to select from, including public transit, taxis, ride-sharing services, and renting automobiles or bikes. Tourists should plan their trips in advance, negotiate rates with taxi drivers, and be careful of their surroundings while utilizing public transit. With a little forethought, travelers can easily move about Rio and see everything the city has to offer.

Chapter 9

Safety and Health

Although it is a popular location, it is necessary to be aware of the safety and health risks that exist in the city. Here are some basic safety precautions for tourists, information about health and medical services in Rio de Janeiro, and emergency contacts and resources.

General Safety Recommendations for Travelers

- **Be careful of your surroundings:** As in any other city, it is crucial to be aware of your surroundings and keep a lookout for anything unusual.

- **Avoid wearing dazzling jewelry or carrying big quantities of money**: This might make you a target for thieves, particularly in busy settings.

- **Utilize official taxis or ride-sharing services**: Unauthorized taxis may be risky, so it's better to stick with licensed taxis or ride-sharing services like Uber or Lyft.

- **Be cautious on the beach:** Although Rio de Janeiro's beaches are lovely, they may also be deadly. Be mindful to heed any caution signs or flags provided by lifeguards.

- **Don't go out alone at night:** It's usually better to travel in groups, particularly at night.

- **Be aware of scams:** Scams are widespread in tourist regions, so be cautious of people giving you discounts that seem too good to be true.

- **Put vital papers and valuables in a secure location**: Keep your passport, ID, and other important documents in a safe place, such as a hotel safe.

Health and Medical Services

Rio de Janeiro has a robust healthcare system, with several public and private hospitals and clinics. Therefore, it is necessary to carry travel insurance to cover any medical expenditures that may emerge.

In case of a medical emergency, there are various hospitals that offer 24-hour emergency treatment, including:

- Hospital Copa D'Or - R. Figueiredo Magalhães, 875 - Copacabana, Rio de Janeiro - RJ, 22031-011, Brazil

- Hospital São Lucas - Rua Siqueira Campos, 143, Copacabana, Rio de Janeiro - RJ, 22031-071, Brazil

- Hospital Quinta D'Or - Rua Almirante Baltazar, 435 - São Cristóvão, Rio de Janeiro - RJ, 20941-010, Brazil

It is also a good idea to have a list of any prescription drugs you are taking, as well as the contact information for your healthcare practitioner back home.

Emergency Contacts and Resources

In case of an emergency, the following phone numbers may be used to receive help:

- Police - 190

- Fire Department - 193

- Ambulance - 192

- Tourist Police - +55 (21) 2332-2924

- American Citizen Services - +55 (21) 3823-2000

Also, it is always a good idea to have the contact information for your embassy or consulate in Rio de Janeiro, as they may give aid in case of an emergency.

Although Rio de Janeiro is a wonderful city to visit, it is vital to take measures and be aware of the safety and health risks that exist. By following these basic safety precautions for tourists, being aware of the health and medical services available, and knowing emergency contacts and resources, you may have a safe and wonderful vacation to Rio de Janeiro.

Chapter 10

Tips for Travelers

With its colorful culture, stunning beaches, and friendly people, Rio offers something for everyone. But, like with any vacation location, there are some things that tourists should bear in mind to guarantee a safe and happy journey. In this chapter, I will present some guidelines for visitors visiting Rio de Janeiro, encompassing basic safety precautions, cultural etiquette, necessary Portuguese words, packing recommendations, and other valuable information.

General Safety Recommendations for Travelers

Be aware of your surroundings: It is crucial to be aware of your surroundings at all times. Rio de Janeiro has certain locations that are deemed more hazardous than others, therefore it is necessary to be vigilant and avoid any areas that look risky.

Avoid carrying big quantities of money or precious items: Pickpocketing and theft are widespread in Rio de Janeiro, therefore it is crucial to keep your belongings secure. Try not to take big quantities of money or expensive objects with you when you go out, and keep your bags and pockets zipped up and close to your body.

Utilize only licensed taxis: Only use licensed taxis when you need to move about the city. Unlicensed taxis, known as "pirate cabs," may be unsafe and may demand outrageous fees.

Be careful while using ATMs: ATM fraud is frequent in Rio de Janeiro, thus it is vital to be cautious when using ATMs. Try to utilize ATMs that are situated within banks or other secure places, and always cover the keypad while entering your PIN.

Remain in well-lit locations: Avoid strolling in dark and secluded regions, particularly at night. Stay to well-lit locations and busy streets, and avoid walking alone whenever feasible.

Cultural Etiquette and Norms

Dress correctly: Rio de Janeiro is a beach city, but it is vital to dress adequately in other regions. While visiting religious places or government facilities, for example, it is vital to dress modestly and properly.

Learn some Portuguese: Although many people in Rio de Janeiro speak English, it is always welcomed when tourists make an effort to learn some Portuguese. Learn some fundamental words such as "hello," "thank you," and "excuse me."

Respect local customs: Rio de Janeiro has a rich cultural legacy, and it is necessary to observe local customs and traditions. For example, it is considered disrespectful to decline food or drink that is provided to you.

Be conscious of personal space: Brazilians prefer to stand near to each other while conversing, so don't be shocked if someone stands close to you. Yet, it is crucial to be cognizant of personal space and not to touch or embrace someone without their agreement.

Essential Portuguese Phrases:

- Olá (oh-LAH) - Hello

- Tudo bem? (TOO-doo behn) - How are you?
- Obrigado/a (oh-bree-GAH-doh/dah) - Thank you
- Por favor (pohr fah-VOHR) - Please
- Desculpe (deh-SKOO-pi) - Forgive me
- Quanto custa? (KWAN-too KOOSH-tah) - How much does it cost?
- Onde fica? (OHN-deh FEE-kah) - Where is it?
- Eu não falo Português (ayoo nah-o FAH-loo por-too-GEHSH) - I don't speak Portuguese.

Packing Advice & Recommendations

If you're considering a vacation to Rio de Janeiro, it's crucial to prepare correctly for the city's tropical temperature and cultural events. **Here are some packing ideas and advice to get the most out of your trip:**

Clothing: Bring lightweight and breathable clothes, such as cotton or linen, for the warm and humid atmosphere. Rio is famed for its beach culture, so be sure to carry a swimsuit, flip flops or sandals, and a beach towel. But, also bring some modest attire for cultural places such as churches, which need covered shoulders and knees.

Sun protection: The sun may be harsh in Rio, so carry sunscreen with a high SPF, sunglasses, and a hat to protect your skin and eyes.

Mosquito protection: Zika virus and other mosquito-borne diseases have become a worry in Brazil. Carry bug repellant with DEET, long-sleeved shirts, and trousers for nighttime wear.

Currency and documents: Carry cash and a credit card, but be careful about exhibiting them in public. Make duplicates of crucial papers like passports and store them in a different location from the originals.

Language: Portuguese is the predominant language in Brazil, therefore it's important to learn some fundamental phrases before your trip. English is spoken in tourist regions but not as commonly outside of those places.

Safety: Rio has a reputation for crime, so it's vital to take measures, such as not carrying precious goods in public and avoiding particular neighborhoods at night. Ask your hotel or hostel for safety tips and suggestions.

Culture: Brazil is famed for its colorful culture, so pack comfortable shoes for dancing, as well as a camera to record the colorful street scenes and cultural acts.

By preparing wisely and being cognizant of the local culture and safety, you may have a good time in Rio de Janeiro. Enjoy your travels!

Dos and Don'ts

Like any major city, there are certain dos and don'ts that tourists should be aware of to ensure a safe and pleasurable vacation. **Here are some tips:**

Dos

- Do see the main tourist sights such as the Christ the Redeemer monument, Sugarloaf Mountain, and Copacabana Beach.

- Do take care to keep yourself and your stuff secure. Be careful of pickpockets, particularly in busy locations, and avoid wandering alone at night in less frequented regions.

- Do sample the native cuisine, such as feijoada and churrasco, and explore the city's thriving culinary scene.

- Do learn some Portuguese words to assist you converse with locals.

- Do respect the local norms and traditions, such as dressing modestly while visiting religious places.

Don'ts
- Don't showcase riches or valuable stuff, such as jewelry or gadgets, since it might make you a target for theft.

- Don't leave your valuables unattended, particularly on the beach.

- Don't carry significant sums of cash with you. Use credit cards or withdraw modest amounts of cash from ATMs as required.

- Don't venture into favelas (shantytowns) without a guide or local resident. These regions might be harmful for travelers.
- Avoid consuming tap water. Use a water filter or only drink bottled water.

By following these dos and don'ts, you may have a safe and pleasurable vacation to Rio de Janeiro.

Conclusion

Rio de Janeiro is a lively city that provides a unique blend of magnificent natural beauty, vibrant culture, and exhilarating nightlife. As a traveler, you will be immersed in a world of samba, soccer, and magnificent beaches that will leave you breathless. With so much to see and do, it's easy to feel overwhelmed, **so, I've put together some last thoughts and ideas to help make your Rio de Janeiro travel experience special.**

Plan ahead: Rio de Janeiro is a vast city with a lot to see and do. To make the most of your time, it's crucial to prepare ahead and select your must-see locations. Make careful to investigate the best attractions and design an itinerary that matches your interests.

Be careful of safety: Although Rio de Janeiro is a beautiful location, it's necessary to be aware of safety problems. Avoid wandering alone at night, particularly in more remote locations, and be alert of pickpockets and other possible frauds. Go to well-lit, crowded locations and don't carry big quantities of cash or costly stuff.

Take use of public transit: Rio de Janeiro has an extensive public transportation system, including buses and metro lines. Using public transit is not only handy, but it's also a terrific method to save money on transportation expenditures.

Enjoy the food: Brazilian cuisine is varied and tasty, with a range of dishes that represent the country's cultural influences. Make sure to taste traditional meals like feijoada, a substantial stew made with black beans and beef, and churrasco, a grilled meat dish that is popular across the nation.

Enjoy the outdoors: Rio de Janeiro is famed for its spectacular natural beauty, and there are lots of options to go out and explore. Take a trek to the summit of Sugarloaf Mountain or Corcovado to view the famed Christ the Redeemer monument. You may also spend a day at one of the numerous gorgeous beaches in and around the city.

Enjoy the culture: Rio de Janeiro is a city with a rich cultural history, and there are lots of possibilities to explore the local culture. Watch a samba concert or visit one of the numerous museums and cultural institutes in the city to learn more about the history and customs of Brazil.

Enjoy the nightlife: Rio de Janeiro is recognized for its active nightlife, with a range of pubs, clubs, and music venues to satisfy all preferences. Make sure to check out the Lapa district, which is renowned for its active nightlife scene.

In conclusion, Rio de Janeiro is a city that provides everything for everyone. With its stunning beaches, rich culture, and vibrant nightlife, it's easy to understand why it's such a popular destination. By preparing ahead, remaining safe, and enjoying the local culture, you're sure to have a wonderful time in this lovely city.

Happy Travels!

Printed in Great Britain
by Amazon